# How To Find Y

## The Right People For You

KIV Books

Copyright © 2017

**Copyright © 2017 KIV Books**

All rights reserved. This book or any portion thereof may not be reproduced or used in any manner whatsoever without the express written permission of the publisher except for the use of brief quotations in a book review.

**Disclaimer**

This book is designed to provide condensed information. It is not intended to reprint all the information that is otherwise available, but instead to complement, amplify and supplement other texts. You are urged to read all the available material, learn as much as possible and tailor the information to your individual needs.

Every effort has been made to make this book as complete and as accurate as possible. However, there may be mistakes, both typographical and in content. Therefore, this text should be used only as a general guide and not as the ultimate source of information. The purpose of this book is to educate.

The author or the publisher shall have neither liability nor responsibility to any person or entity regarding any loss or damage caused, or alleged to have been caused, directly or indirectly, by the information contained in this book.

# Table of Contents

INTRODUCTION .................................................................................. 5

CHAPTER 1: OUT WITH THE OLD, IN WITH THE NEW ....................... 7

CHAPTER 2: TELL ME WHO YOUR FRIENDS ARE ............................. 11

CHAPTER 3: TRIAL AND ERROR ........................................................ 15

CHAPTER 4: TRUST AND CONFIDENCE ............................................ 19

CHAPTER 5: BE THE TRIBE MEMBER YOU WANT ............................ 23

CHAPTER 6: THE PRIORITY GAME .................................................... 27

CHAPTER 7: E FOR EFFORT ............................................................... 31

CHAPTER 8: LIFE'S TREASURES ........................................................ 35

CHAPTER 9: #TRIBEWORLD ............................................................. 39

CHAPTER 10: THE TIME IS NOW ...................................................... 43

# Introduction

In an ever changing and exclusive "me" world it is increasingly difficult to find people that would be our permanent group of friends. It is hard to even imagine a squad that won't change members every so often.

But what if you aren't the type to move out of your comfort zone? What if it is hard for you to make new friends? Are you going to just do things on your own or are you going to suffer in silence around people who don't really get you?

The answer is NEITHER. You have to find a way to be able to gain the kind of friendships that would be lasting and meaningful. You have to find, make and grow your tribe.

First you need to figure out what a tribe means in this day and age. The traditional meaning is a group of dwellers who grew up together in the same culture and speak a similar language. But that is not the kind of tribe that we are going to talk about here. You have to expand the meaning of that word and go ahead and identify the kind of people whom you want to have in your life.

There are a lot of challenges involved in bringing people into your life. There would be some heartbreak when you have to let people go too. But all the experiences that you would have would give you a solid group of people who would be there willing to grow old with you and share their lives with you. And it would be all worth all the effort you put into it.

# Chapter 1: Out with the Old, In with the New

*"Make new friends, but keep the old; Those are silver, these are gold."*

- Joseph Parry

Most people start off finding new friends by abandoning their old ones. That is not always the smartest thing to do. You need to make an assessment of how relevant those people are to your life. Ask yourself if their loss would impact you negatively and in which ways. If the effects are more positive than it is negative, do not hesitate to let go of some people.

Who should you let go?

First on the list are emotional vampires. How can you spot one? This person or so-called friend likes to basically rain on everyone's parade. They suck the happiness of the room with just their general attitude and behavior. It is possible that you stuck around this person because another friend of yours is their friend too. So you had to put up with them and so never had a chance to filter them out for fear that your actual friend would be inconvenienced.

What should you do to get rid of emotional vampires? You either stop them from being that way which is akin to changing the key defense mechanism of that person and then stay friends with them. But it is harder for these people to be positive thinkers. They always focus on their own needs and emotions rather than others.

There are more than enough incidents when this person has caused you discomfort or shame. Having them around makes you use up more energy in trying to go with what they need. They are so needy that you find yourself catering to them more often than you cater to your needs.

In this case you are the enabler. Incidentally, you should not have too many of these in your tribe. Make sure to have one or two who can push people to action but not the kind who would let people get away with something illegal.

Although they are often in the background, enablers can be the kind that can make or break a tribe. If you let too many in, sure there would be a lot of activity but there would also be a lot of unfinished plans because they are not good in being firm about a deadline. We need a friend who supports us in all the things that we want to do. But the enabler would not veto the bad things and just let you make so many mistakes that are not necessary.

Drama queens/princes are the types that you really should avoid. They treat you like a lady in waiting or a second-class friend. They don't care about your schedule and they are supposed to always get their way. The one thing that you need to tell this person is NO. When you feel even a bit of doubt and you have other things you need to do, just say no.

Your plans and needs are as important as that person's and you don't have to always accommodate them. Do not fold. If they still want to be part of your tribe, they wouldn't mind the new assertiveness that you found. After all, you are entitled to positive change.

There are other smaller types of people that might irk you. Reflect and assess on what those people mean to you. One thing that you can do is go through your social media list and list down the people whom you like or dislike. Do not put a maybe on your list. Just two lists.

Then check the list of the people you like, cross out anyone you do not talk to in person or send messages to on social media. From what are left behind, cross out anyone you would message personally if there was a death in your family. Those are the people you would reach out to when you are in your worst state. Among these people are potential members of your core tribe.

After finding out what kind of people you have to let go, you should make sure that you think about the people who are missing in your squad. Get together with your friends and sort out what kind of people are ideally missing in your tribe.

And if they know someone who they think would be a good addition to your group. Then set up a gathering. Don't do something as intimate as a plain coffee get-together because that new person might not be able to keep up with the stories that you all share. It would be best to go somewhere that would require more group activities than intimate one on one question and answer.

What if you end up with nobody after you have sorted out the people who were making your life toxic? Be brave. Don't fall back into old habits and settle for who is available at the moment. That is how you ended up with the wrong people in the first place.

Consider this as a new chapter in your life. Meeting new people is difficult if you are on the meek side. But it is actually a great adventure that could lead you to discovering more about yourself. Now that you are not compromising your wishes and giving up on what you really need, you have a new found lease on life. And the people you will meet this time would be on purpose.

So enjoy the ride and don't let regret pull you back to your old so-called tribe.

# Chapter 2: Tell Me Who Your Friends Are

*"No person is your friend who demands your silence, or denies your right to grow."*

*- Alice Walker*

The fact that you now want to choose the right people to be a part of your life, means you need to know ONE person the most, the FUTURE YOU. You need to know what kind of person you want to be in the future and why that is your choice. Then you should reach out to people who would be useful in your life in the future. If the people you used to have in your life would be relevant in your future, keep them.

The people that you welcome in your life need to be present and not the kind who you would just meet once in a while and keep in your contact list to rot. Make active contacts that are going to emphasize the good things in their lives and share them with you.

Those who are willing to understand that you are not always going to be actively participating in their daily lives but trust that you would be there when they need you the most and vice versa. When we are younger, we want to have friends who are always physically present.

But as we grow older, we need to understand that you are going to have to fit friends in our schedule and not burden them with too many abrupt plans. Because the members of our tribe would drop whatever they are doing to be at our side when we need them. So we need to make sure that our calls for help are the ones that are worth the bother.

The people you keep from the old would still influence the new people you meet. So you have to make sure that the friends you kept are welcoming of new people. The main issue that you might have is if they do not mix together well. And if you are not able to compartmentalize your group of friends, you tribes might clash. You might end up having to choosing between the two and that would be extremely difficult.

That is where your present self would be tested. The kind of person that you are will surface every time you are in a hectic situation. Knowing what you prioritize is going to make it that much easier to choose the people in your tribe.

For the most part tribe members are like your family apart from your actual one. Because they are the people who you want to share everything with. In a world where almost everyone just brags about what they have online, showing one's flaws have increasingly become difficult.

We don't want to show our vulnerabilities to anyone. Tribe members make it easy for us to share the things that we find confusing. And we are not afraid that they would judge us for our misgivings. They accept who we are but do not let us stop growing.

They are don't push us out of comfort zones but nudge us slowly until we eventually take that one step over that line. And sometimes we are not even aware of it. Those people just live their lives as an example. We don't envy them in the conventional way that people do. We want the core values of their happiness and admire them for their resolve. These are the kind of influencers who motivate us to have a better life just because they want us to genuinely be happy.

Many times in the search for tribe members we would stumble upon people who want to mold us into the kind of friend or tribe members who they think fits THEIR status in society. They would initially say that it is for our own good. And they would make a lot of sense because they are intelligent and very convincing. But not all changes are for the self-improvement of the friend but a reflection of their own prejudice.

But how do you know that this is being done to you when it is so subtle? It starts pretty small. When you start feeling like the changes around you are a bit too stiff for your own taste. It is when your suggestions start to get put off in the most sarcastic ways. When your idea becomes considered cheap or belittled for their lack of class, you should start getting the hint.

You will start to do things with that friend that you really don't want to do. And then they expect you to adjust your palette, budget and time just to do that thing that you really never wanted to do. And when this happens repeatedly, either the same activity or another similar to it in context, you need to remember that you have the right to say no. Often when these kind of conversations start, the person who is looking down on you would say that they are just giving you either a lesson on culture or life.

At that time, do not be afraid to speak out and say that you don't need either one. It could be as simple as the act of drinking wine. If you already said that you don't like it for any reason and they still insist on you trying it over and over, it is time to put your foot down.

If they start to make you feel small and ridicule you for any change or new thing you do not wish to do, do not be afraid to walk away. Those who are your true friends and want to keep you in their lives won't be afraid to come after you and talk it out. Those who consider you dispensable wouldn't even be bothered by you literally walking away from them.

It would hurt when that realization hits you that the people who you made time for just consider you as a buffer so they won't be bored with just a handful of friends around them. But you have to be strong since those people will continue on their lives judging everyone in their wake.

It is not just you who becomes their victim. It is not your responsibility to change that aspect of their personality. They are like sharks that need to keep swimming in order to breathe. As for you, move away from their range and heal yourself.

This is not to mean that you become petrified into the person that you are now. List down the things you heard people say about you and make a list of the things you should improve on. Ask your core friends about those things and identify things from easiest to do to hardest.

Your definition of easy and hard might be different from those of others at this point. So you should decide the order of things to do. Because the change would directly change your life not theirs, so the pace should meet your needs and abilities.

# Chapter 3: Trial and Error

*"Choose your friends wisely – they will make or break you"*

*- J. Willard Marriott*

When you encounter people for the first time, a first impression forms quickly and often without us even being aware that we were forming it. And the rest of the time that we know that person, the things we learn about them, the conversations we have with them would chip at that first impression until all that we really have is the person who we know them as.

This is not always the true personality of that person. Unless we are unbelievably good at reading people and we have been with that person every minute of the day since we first met them, we won't know who that person really is. And we have to be okay with that.

Most people feel insecure around strangers because of the fear of the unknown. We feel awkward because we don't know how our words and actions would be received. But that is where the need for personal growth and bonding time comes in. We can't really know one person, not even a lover of many years, but we can try our hardest to do so.

If we truly want them to be part of our life's tribe then it is imperative that we put in the time and the effort. The resulting relationship would shape our future.

The kind of friendships and relationships that we gain from our effort would bring us a lot of joy especially in the sunnier times of our lives. We share experiences and learn new things together. Everything is an adventure.

But just like dating, there are times when the happiness fades and we must put in more effort to make things work. Real friends don't end their friendship after a single fight. They don't ignore each other just because it would make it more comfortable for the other person. It is when they talk it out and make sure that they have said their piece.

And at the end of that conversation there is either a compromise or an agreement to disagree. We can be friends with people who have similar tastes or hobbies but we are ultimately different from each other. There are times when too much familiarity can also cause problems. We are so used to each other that we automatically assume they would understand what we are saying or why we are doing certain things.

But people have relatively different worries and situations at every given time. They might be a good friend but at the moment when you were dumping all your worries at their feet, they were barely even able to juggle their own worries as well. We need to be sensitive to what the other person is able to handle. That doesn't always mean that you keep things from that friend since that can hurt them too.

But you have to know the art of timing when it comes to building a friendship. Make sure that you respect the time they need to reach out. Don't nag them that they should have come to you earlier. If they come to you for a problem, do not ask how many other people knew before you did. It is not a popularity contest. All that matters is that they are there, broken or out of focus with their lives and they need you.

The same way that we need to be needed by others in order to have a full-filling live, the need to be loved and accepted is ingrained in us. We know that people would always be there for us and we also want to be needed by those people. Value goes around in that manner. But do not mistake this with being too dependent on those people.

They should help you become a person who can handle your life on your own. Friends are not troubleshooters, bartenders or emergency contacts. They are people who are supposed to be there through both bright and dark days. They should be willing to be there for both. Those who only want to stick around when things are sunny but walk off with your umbrella during stormy life moments, are the ones you should avoid or let go.

How do you avoid those people? Honestly, you can't. Because you can spend many years being a friend to one person and then when the major life event happens they bail. That is the only time you would know who your real friends are.

And it is the worst time for it too. But that is the truth of it. When the world seems to be crashing around you, the ones who help you stay on your feet are the ones whose friendships would last for a lifetime. They won't care if you have flaws and are not always able to do the same things that they can. But they understand only one thing at that moment. "My friend needs me."

And finding friends like these is all trial and error. We meet different people in our lives and we can't filter them all. Although quite interestingly, we can learn how those people would act if we are in unusual situations. You can ask them what they would do if something happens to you. Listen in not on the complementary answers. Look for the sincere answers. Most often than not, that person would say something that is not always pleasant but true.

Do not surround yourself with echo-type people. Those who just sound off whatever you are telling them. Have friends who are opinionated. They are the kind who would tell you things as they are. And they would not sugarcoat it just to make you feel better. Just by being around their sincerity should already make you feel confident that they are not just saying those things to put you down.

Friends who shoot down an idea you have should explain why. If they can't be bothered to explain it, then that person is just shooting it down due to their own prejudices. Real friends take time to flesh things out. They stretch coffee dates and let it spill into drinks just because they know you need the time to figure things out.

They are focused in their lives but their schedule is flexible when it comes to important times like these. Don't judge them for the words they want you to ponder on. Reserve your judgment of the result. If you do not try something just because of laziness, that isn't good enough.

You have to try something because you need to do it, not just because your friend said you should do it. The changes it would make in your life would be different simply because you are a different person than you friend.

How do you deal with the heartbreak that is cause by an ending friendship? You can let out as much tears as you need to mourn a lost connection. Friends of more than a decade are difficult to lose because you feel like a part of your past gets erased if you do that. That is not true.

Who you are now was shaped by that past. So your past never really disappears. We live a continuation of the mistakes that we did and the solutions we applied to our problems. Things are always constantly changing, even the people we rely on do. So we must know how to let go of someone who is deadweight in our lives

Just because you have known each other for a long time doesn't give them the right to walk all over you and the dreams you have of your future.

Make it simple. Think of yourself on a porch of a nursing home or your own home when you are retired. While you are doing something to pass the time while talking, who are the people around you? If that person doesn't even come close to your list of friends by that point, make an active decision to let that friend just be an acquaintance or grow an even deeper friendship. It is all up to you.

# Chapter 4: Trust and Confidence

*"A friend is one who walks in when others walk out"*

*- Walter Winchell*

How do you make a tribe of the best people you know become a life goal? Simple, just be the glue.

We all have that one friend who seems to be the center of your friendships with other people. Regardless of where you met that person, people tend to end up in your circle of friends because of your association with her.

This is often beneficial if you are a timid person. You are exposed to more people because people tend to gravitate towards him or her. It can be overwhelming but you learn to cope because you have confidence that you can trust your friend to help you.

Most people think that the glue is someone who is extroverted and engaged. But for the most part, the glue of a group or a tribe is a wise person. That person can be an extrovert or an introvert. It just so happens that the wise person is willing to share their time and knowledge to all the people in the tribe. The glue has the ability to make a stubborn member of the tribe come out of their self-imposed hibernation.

They know what buttons to press in order for the members of a tribe to act in the right way. But they do not abuse this advantage. They already know that it works both ways. They are as vulnerable as they are influential. They feel the need to use this ability only during emergencies. If the person who knows all your secrets uses them all the time to make you do things you dislike.

That person is not being the glue but being a bully. They are weaponizing your fears and secrets and that is not fair to you or the confidence that revelation was made on.

The secrets we share with tribe members are often things we can't even tell our family members. Sometimes we need someone who isn't willing to judge us based on blood to be able to open up. And with this comes a great amount of trust. We are hoping that the person we trust won't break our trust.

Is it possible to make sure that the tribe members we choose are trust-worthy? It is possible to do this, to some extent. Unfortunately, the person we gave our trust to can also make mistakes that would lead them to reveal some of the things we told them in confidence.

Some people would try to combat against this by putting the secret of that person for all to see. But this kind of retaliation isn't going to fix anything. Talking it out with the person would reveal whether or not the secret was spilled accidentally or intentionally. You have to at the very least give them the benefit of the doubt. If you let yourself be swept by the moment, then you might lose a good friend over a misunderstanding.

If the person still chooses to lie to your face, then you have every right to cut ties with them. You should not walk on eggshells in a friendship. It is no longer a friendship if that is the case.

Whatever trust you expect to gain from others, you must earn with effort. Make sure that you do the right thing by your tribe mates. Deal with them with sincerity. People who return sincerity with malice are the types who shouldn't last in your tribe.

They would turn others against each other. They thrive on chaos. It might be because they want people to pay attention to them. It could also be caused by jealousy. They don't want others to have a better disposition than they do. And they take out their frustration on others. Don't let people like this break your friendships.

Can you be the glue and not be the peacemaker? Yes and no. Most of the time the glue acts as the hub of the tribe since they know what is happening with everyone. They make it a point to keep in touch with everyone. So oftentimes they can relay the information to others in the tribe. The glue can take the backseat when it comes to fights.

They might let the concerned parties talk it out amongst themselves and only act or speak when asked for their opinion about the situation. They are not going to take sides and that might upset the people who are arguing. But that is their main task, to keep the two sides together even if they refuse to acknowledge each other. They believe in people even when they themselves already gave up on each other.

# Chapter 5: Be the Tribe Member You Want

*"Share our similarities, celebrate our differences."*

*- M.Scott Peck*

Most people want to have tribe mates that are top notch. This isn't a pipe dream only if you are also a person that would attract these kinds of people. If you are a goal-oriented person, then others like you would be able to find you. The main thing about this is action. Once you move into gear to get your life on track, the people who would improve it would be easier to reach. If you are pushing for a change that is not good for you, you are most likely going to face obstacles – both internally and externally.

If you are the kind of person who gives up easily, then you won't find people who are braver and bolder than you. That is simply because you find difficult situations to be a bother. You can't move in the circle of the people who might be the best ones to find and include in your tribe if you are not willing to make sacrifices related to your personal space.

Your prejudices can also hold you back. Thinking that only a certain group of people would be a good source of tribe members will be your biggest regret. Diversity breeds so much creativity that the ideas you can get from them would be endless. And if you are the type to want to get your tribe mates together to build an actual business, then diversity would lead to a lot of interesting products and services that you can't think up all on your own.

There is a significant amount of self-reflection that needs to be done by a person who wants to have a lot of new tribe members in their life. There are a lot of things that we want to do that others might not be willing to do. But convincing someone that you are worth their time as a friend and as an associate would defend on one thing: self-development.

Real winners do not stop growing. And the best you would be a person who is able to accept change quickly and positively. There is not one person in the world who likes to change something that they are already used to. It is scary and taxing.

But the attitude towards change can lead to positive results. If we do not fear change, then meeting a new person wouldn't be as scary. It would be something normal and necessary. Because the more positive energy and people we have in our lives, the more effective we are in making improvements in our personal and professional life.

More and more these days, we turn to our friends or tribe mates when deciding on which changes to enact in our lives. From the very simple task of choosing a new outfit to the more life-altering career choices, we all need the input of the people we consider as our life mentors.

We often pick and choose these people among the ones we usually hang out with. They are the people who we believe know us well and can challenge us to do something. We also value their input with it comes to the pros and cons of a new environment. Since we trust their judgment, we seek it.

In order for us to be the tribe mate that we would want, we must constantly exchange information with others. And the abundant number of acquaintances can be considered one valuable tribe mate. Sometimes there are just things that "our people" do not have the information for. This is when well-connected tribe mates come in handy.

We all need that one friend who always knows a person who does a certain thing. Their network becomes your network by extension. So if you are an introverted person, find your own network of geniuses who can give you solid advice on something. If you are uncomfortable with changing experts in each field, make an effort to eliminate the people your friends do not recommend.

But keep in mind that experience is the best teacher and what might not be good for one person works for you. So try to at least check the reviews over any service before you eliminate them from the choices. Remember that people have prejudices too.

That is the same for people. Do not eliminate them just because they don't seem to be as clean and shiny as the other friends you already have. As previously mentioned, diversity can also make your group of friends invaluable.

The search for the perfect friend is a eluding as the search for the best partner in life. There isn't a perfect person who can check all the things on our perfect friend list. That is just the ideal. Sometimes, the person who becomes so valuable to us is actually someone who isn't even checking out any of the things on our list. If we box people into types, we run the risk of pushing away really good people.

Be open but alert. The way we communicate with each other has many edit options and filters. Try to find the kind of people who would be genuine not just with you. Remember that what seems too good to be true might just be. Inspire sincerity in people.

And know that you are going to be much better off if you are honest about your feelings. People always think that hiding the truth to keep someone from getting hurt is better. But the truth always comes out. And the fact that you kept something painful yet valuable from that person adds to their pain.

Be the kind of tribe mate who shares not just material gifts but the gift of understanding and trust.

# Chapter 6: The Priority Game

*"Nobody is too busy. It's just a matter of priorities."*

*- Anonymous*

Now let's say that you already found some tribe members. It's easy to meet with them if there are only a handful of them. But what happens when the number is doubled or tripled. Do you eliminate anyone now that they have become invaluable to you?

You don't. You manage your time and your life by this point and make sure that all tribe members do not feel like you don't need them anymore. If they are truly part of your tribe, you should make time for them.

Most of the really busy individuals would raise an eyebrow at this and say that they can barely make time for themselves. That is the wrong way to think about having free time. Free time isn't the gaps that we have in our schedules. Free time isn't the time you can save when you take shortcuts and make lists. Free time is the time we actively set aside for something important apart from work and business endeavors.

Whenever you get an invitation these days, you reach for your online or phone calendar to check if your schedule can accomodate it. The annoying thing is when you don't have anything to do last weekend but all of a sudden the next weekend is full of events you have to attend. And choosing which one is more important is daunting.

Most of the time it is best to choose life events over things that can be put off. Once of a lifetime events are important as they can no longer be replicated in the same scale. But make sure that you explain to the other tribe members you have to turn down why you are choosing the life event over their invitation. If they are true tribe members, they would understand you.

Don't downplay the importance of the event you chose just to make them feel good. Why? Word can reach the other tribe members easily. If you say that you don't really want to go to your family member's wedding it could cause a irreparable rift between you and that person.

It is hard to choose but not choosing is even worse. Why? Because you would add two things to your regret list rather than just one. If you choose to be neutral, nobody gets to see you and both invitations are wasted. The sentiment and affection that is attached to that invitation would also be lost. Next time they want people to come to a celebration or a life event, you won't be a priority because they'd remember that slight.

People who can't keep their promises are the worst kind. When it is you who is making the promise, don't be vague. That can lead to a lot of misunderstandings. If you are more direct, there might be pain from the rejection but at the very least they are not hoping for nothing. A lack of memories is more haunting than having good and bad memories mixed together.

Don't say yes to everything. Do not double book events or invitations. Prioritizing can help make the quality of the experience go up. There are not a lot of chances to always see people who have hectic schedules. And you are not the only one who made adjustments.

Other people in the tribe must have done the same thing. So you can't just complain the whole time that you did your best to make it to that get-together. It dampens the mood when you highlight the possible repercussions of your action when you come back to work or see the other friend whom you turned down. Own up to your choice.

Expect the same from the people in your tribe. It would be harder once you grow older together. Priorities shift so most of the time, younger years seems so nostalgic because it was easier to get everyone to agree and faster. Don't use the same scheduling tactics you used when people were unattached or childless. The kind of activities you would do would also change. It is harder for single members of the tribe to see the married members because they have lesser things in common and the gap is hard to bridge at times.

The married members should remember that it should be balanced. The single ones should not always be the ones to adjust. If the city dwellers and the suburban dwellers need to meet, go somewhere in the middle. Discover new places to go to and find meet-up spots where they can bring their families as well as enjoy themselves.

Compromise is the best solution for everything. Do not give up half-way just because scheduling is hard. Don't make the person who was not there feel bad. That is not the goal of meeting up with friends. It is to connect not to alienate. Technology now allows for the inclusion of someone who is not physically there.

So you can allow that person to join in the spirit of things by showing them what you are doing at a given time. It would be hard to do it the whole time. But at the very least the feeling of "wish you were here" is positive and not "you missed something awesome".

As much as you might want to always be present in every gathering, this is impossible. But be understanding and don't keep score of their attendance. That would make them feel like your friendship is a class they have to pass.

If you are the one who can't go, make sure that you are not just putting it off because you don't feel like doing something. Often when we just want to be couch potatoes, our mind actually needs active stimuli. So go out and do something with your friends. It would be lost time.

# Chapter 7: E for Effort

*"No frienship is an accident."*

*- O. Henry, Heart of the West*

In order to make good tribe mates stick around, you have to make an effort. It is not just about giving them something. It is definitely not about being at their beck and call. It is the value of the interaction that would matter. Making deliberate plans to include them in your daily life is key. You don't have to be the birthday diva to remember everyone's birthday. That is what refrigerator calendars and phone calendars are for.

One thing that you can do is to make two alarms for someone's birthday on your schedule. One should be for midnight, so you can send them a note or a message on their birthday and the other one is to place a possible alert on what you are going to do for them on their birthday.

It doesn't have to be a big thing. It can even just be a cup of coffee after work or sending a cake to them for that day. They say that the thought counts, it is actually the EFFORT that counts.

So if you are the kind of person who forgets things like birthdays and anniversaries use technology to help you. Place it on EVERYTHING so that you won't forget it. Put it on your phone calendar, your online calendar and the paper desk calendar you have at work or in your home.

Post-Its are your best friend. Color-code birthday of tribe mates using your favorite color so that your eyes go towards it when you see it. If you are the paper organizer type, make sure that you make a habit to check things daily on it. Put a "week before" entry on your organizer so that you don't panic regarding what gift to get.

If you know that you would have a lot on your plate for the quarter, do a group buy for gifts. That saves a trip to the store that you would have to fit in your schedule when everything else is already occupying your time. If you don't buy things in a hurry, you might end up with fewer expenses than a rushed trip to the mall.

Small things also add up to become a habit. You should make sure to not just check up on someone when you have free time. Take a look at how they are doing and reach out in the morning. Most people might find it a bit odd that you suddenly start sending bible quotes or quotable quotes to them so early in the morning. But make it something consistent and they might end up looking forward to it.

Do not underestimate the simple fact that people might not be getting any messages from anyone at all that day. And your tiny act of including them to a group message or a text message could lift someone's spirit.

We think that making an effort takes a lot of energy from us. But it actually is a way to energize us. When we have a purpose for our day, things we do are deliberate and not routine. Routine can cause stress too. So make sure to go out of your way to do something that can break your routine. You get to make someone feel good and you get to do something different. It's a win-win situation.

Be on the lookout for someone who is only willing to be your friend when you give them something. Those leech-types should be cut off before they cause you harm.

Don't expect them to reciprocate. Do not always ask for something in return. Do it for the sake of doing it because it makes you feel good. Your tribe mates are not obligated to give you something else apart from a sincere thank you. That is not to say that you should keep ungrateful people. What you would come to know about true tribe mates is that they can't sit still until they've paid you back for the good you have brought into their lives.

The small things that they would do, appreciate all of them. Sometimes we just expect things from others and we don't show them that we are grateful. Don't ever put it off. Thank who you need to thank at the exact moment you felt gratitude.

Delays can lead to misunderstandings. The next time that person wants to do something for you they might second guess their decision. Often people write off people who seem ungrateful. Don't let shyness cause a problem when there shouldn't be any. It becomes a habit after a while. And it makes you feel better since you know that you have acknowledged the effort of others.

Tribe mates aim to lift the burden from the shoulders of their other tribe mates. If there is a person who only likes to dump their concerns but never listens to others, call them out. Even if a person is in a bad situation, they can still be capable of being compassionate towards another person.

# Chapter 8: Life's Treasures

*"Close friends are truly life's treasures. Sometimes they know us better than we know ourselves. With gentle honesty, they are there to guide and support us, to share our laughter and our tears. Their presence reminds us that we are never really alone."*

*- Vincent Van Gogh*

After all the effort you put in finding the ones who you think fits in your life, and made the effort necessary to keep their in your life, what happens next?

The answer is simple. Life happens next. Whatever life would throw at you, you would have these people to be there for you. They would be the ones who would be there when you are trying to start something new. Making something out of nothing can be daunting. But with tribe mates who would constantly ask you how you are doing, then you would have support.

There are some people who might seem not that valuable in the beginning. Their value won't come to light until you experience something that is too daunting for you to handle. They are not the loudest member or the most engaged person in the tribe. But at times when even the liveliest person can't lift the spirit of tribe members a silent yet sturdy support is vital.

What happens when the person turns away or fades out of your life? Do they still belong in your tribe? Yes and possibly no. Yes, because their value is something that you attach to them. If knowing that they are there give you comfort, then they continue to be tribe members. It likes when elders become part of a group. They might not always be going out and making active decisions. But when things require wisdom and quiet resolve, they are the ones the group turns to.

If a person fades out of your life, there is a reason. And the reason isn't always something that you did. People often wonder if the reason why their friend is not around anymore is because of something that the tribe or the members did. Sometimes that person just wants to go off on their own. They are finding themselves and their purpose.

If they find their purpose then they would find their way back. If their purpose takes them very far from the old tribe, do not take it against them. You are abandoned but you are a part of who they are now. Perhaps being part of your tribe led them to that path of self-discovery.

Being a part of a tribe isn't mandatory or permanent. There are people who we will lose, because of life and because of death. Drifting apart isn't caused by just one side. But them walking away or going to a different path isn't always a bad thing.

We can't hold back anyone from leaving a tribe. Don't let the secrets scared shackle them in the group. Because a person who is adamant in leaving, when forced to stay will turn the group towards each other. They would see that escape is only possible if everything falls apart.

That is not something that you would wish on your tribe or others.

Do not classify your friends and tribe members based on their value or status. Everyone is of equal value. You might have people in the tribe that you are closer to. But that doesn't mean that others should be excluded once you have chosen your favorites. Remember that all of them are your "people". And if you do not treat them fairly, they will leave you. And the loss will cause imbalance in your life.

Even if there is no physical implications - since they are your core tribe –it would cause you stress and discomfort. Most of the time we don't feel the need to go after people who already left yet the impact of the loss is felt belatedly. When something amazing happens and we can't tell a specific person, one we know would appreciate it the most, the happiness is somewhat tainted.

Most of the time when people form groups, they actually monitor the people that are part of their group. If you only formed a group to keep up with the trends of having many friends, you are not forming the right tribe. You should carefully and slowly fill the tribe you are building with invaluable people. If you add people just for the sake of keeping up a number, then you would be left with a lot of regretful encounters.

Be secure and trust that your tribe would survive no matter what. Knowing that you have reliable people, even if your tribe is just a tribe of three should be enough for the time being. You can still make new friends even if you have a core tribe.

Having a tribe doesn't mean you can't meet new people. Life always puts you in the way of other people. And if you get a chance to meet someone who would have potential to be a tribe member, you can always introduce that person to your existing core tribe members.

They say that we should always be on the ready for an adventure. And whatever you style in making new friends, remember never to close your door to possibilities.

Our lifetime is too short to meet everyone in the world, good people come to us and sometimes bad people get a chance to infiltrate our lives. But we must never give up on people in general because of this.

# Chapter 9: #TribeWorld

*"Six degrees of separation doesn't mean that everyone is linked to everyone else in just six steps. It means that a very small number of people are linked to everyone else in a few steps, and the rest of us are linked to the world through those special few."*

*- Malcolm Gladwell, The Tipping Point: How Little Things Can Make a Big Difference*

We are living in a world where connections are added or even prompted by technology. How does this help you find your tribe?

It all depends on how you use it.

Sometimes people who are able to become a part of your tribe are out there in the far reaches of the internet. Some people even find life partners in the same manner.

How hard would it be to identify them and know for sure that their online image is the same as the person they project themselves to be? It would be very hard. But time and more intimate conversations would be helpful in making that decision. A combination of the different mediums of communication would help you. As more and more applications allow for "live" features, you can get unfiltered conversations that are similar to the ones which you can have with someone who lives nearby.

Consider all of those mediums as windows which both of you can use to talk about your lives and share it. The definition of share has become a bit detached because of technology. What we believe we are sharing to our contacts are just something that might scroll down or ignore. Your feed is controlled and filtered to only seek the things that you find easy to relate to.

But this limits your world view and narrows down the chance for discovery. The best thing to do is to diversify event the things that you believe is valuable. So that you can still see things that your more conservative friends or more liberal friends post, you should engage all of them in dialogue. Open the channels for understanding even in your social media.

That way the different kinds of people who might become tribe mates, can find their way to your profile.

Having a channel under which you can share your ideas is vital at this day and age. But more and more people whose opinions we disagree in are scattered in our newsfeed.

The interesting thing is that tribes now thrive in using group chat and messengers to share what is happening in their lives. But a person who shares their lives all the time can also alienate others.

We cannot control how people perceive us. They have their own opinion and prejudices. Even if you are harmlessly posting about the sunset at a beach you were visiting, some may take it as you showing off that you are on vacation for the nth time.

Anything positive you post can be twisted by anyone so it is very important to filter people in your social media and your life. Don't let those who you do not want to hear from have a chance to ruin your day or your memory.

Remember to not engage in an argument with these people. There are options to cancel comments on posts these days. If you think that you just want to say your piece, and if you are not trying to hurt anyone by saying it, go ahead and speak your mind.

But know that even if you mean well, people would say or think however they wish.

If you start filtering your thoughts because of just a handful of people, then set up your account to exclude them. If they ask you why you did it stand up for your choice.

Most people do not add their boss to their social media because they feel like they are being monitored. But you don't need to be monitored if you are professional even online. Remember that talking smack about your boss on social media can always be found out.

If you have a tribe member that you have a problem with, don't use the internet to attain anonymity to get back at them. That doesn't make you better than them if you backstab them with an anonymous post. Nothing stays anonymous because there is a chance that a secret told to you was for your ears only. And so the person would know automatically who the culprit is. You would lose face and perhaps more than one tribe mates.

These days, we can't limit our tribe to people who are in our area or even our country. There are people who can be core members of your tribe without ever having a chance to meet. They say that internet friends are akin to pen pals we never get to see in person. We can share interests with them that people around us don't understand.

It's not necessary to meet someone in person to be their friend. Technology has already made it possible to keep tabs on each other even if we are continents apart. The difference in culture is blurred by common interests. For example two girls who like a particular artist can find each other through a tweet or a post. They can start off as mutual followers and later get a chance to talk about daily life and issues. Hitting it off with a stranger is not that uncommon on the internet. We can meet a lot of people who we can talk to about diverse topics. We can bring in our tribe mates in the conversation. It helps us realize which ones of our tribe mates are truly open-minded.

When a friendship grows in alternative ways, the amount of effort is actually doubled. We have no chance to do activities together so inclusion is best. We can broadcast just about everything we do now. So choose those important moments and allow your important groups of friends to know what you are up to in actual time.

Those who can't be there on time can catch up by watching the replay. They can talk to you about it later and that would be that. You don't have to publicly show all the moments of your life. Just pick a specific moment for each group of people.

Don't let your contact list be riddled with people you never talk to. If those people are really not active on social media, then reach out to them and ask them for their contact information. If they can't be bothered to answer you, let them go. If they can't find time for you, don't bother making time for them. Simple actions speak volumes. Lack of it builds up to neglect.

If you are lucky to find tribe mates online then you must make sure to commit to this friendship with everything you have.

If possible, find a way, through your common interests to travel to a new place together. Meeting your internet friends are a part of the goals list of your friendship. Unless they are living in a war-stricken country or it is too expensive for both of you to ever travel to anywhere, there is always a way to meet.

# Chapter 10: The Time Is Now

*"Always find opportunities to make someone smile, and to offer random acts of kindness in everyday life."*

- Roy T. Bennet, The Light in the Heart

If you want to start a tribe and wondering when is the right time, it's now. The comfort zone that you have been dwelling in for the longest time needs to be expanded. Most people make excuses to do it next time and never actually do it. The time that you spend calculating what you want to do would also take away from time that you can go out and meet new people. Meeting people can also include time online but it's not the same.

You have to have face to face interaction to improve your "tribe-dar". The tribe-dar is this instinct that you can develop over time as you try to get more members in your tribe.

Some people have the natural ability to read people. For the most part it is just because they are focused on details. They can pick out behavior based on the speaking pattern and the movements of people. But for the rest of us, we need time to figure out if the people we meet at are genuine or not.

If you get disheartened easily, try to seek help. Talk to your friends about the people that you meet. It's like having a tribe-wingman or woman. If you share your thoughts about someone to a trusted person, then you can figure out whether you sound too paranoid or unreasonable.

Learn to give chances. Most of the time people are all or nothing when it comes to their trust. Don't be that way when it comes to building your tribe. There should be a considerable amount of chances given to people who you want to have in our tribe.

Understand that tribe members are not supposed to be perfect individuals. They are people who can make mistakes. Unless it is a betrayal of your trust or something illegal, forgiving them shouldn't be too much of a bother. Forgiving them fully is a choice that you have to make.

If you hold grudges then the next time they make a mistake, you would most likely bring it up. Friendships are not supposed to be smooth-sailing all the time. They are a lot of effort and time to build. In the end, there could just be one small thing that can cause the friendship to have a crack.

Don't let these cracks get any bigger or cause any more trouble than they previously did. Patching things up means talking and constantly checking if things are really okay. Setting aside time for your tribe mates is key to having a healthy friendship. Even if it means just one a year seeing them when they come back from another country, don't make excuses and just go.

If you are having a hard time with the current tribe mates that you have, evaluate their worth in your life. Be bold when it comes to your decisions in who to cut out.

It would be tough because other members of your tribe are already intertwined. You run the risk of losing everyone. But it is your life, it is your tribe and you have to decide who is really the tribe mates you want for the rest of your life. Don't settle for mediocre tribe mates and find the best ones for you.

Printed in Great Britain
by Amazon